THE PYTHON PROGRAMMING YOUR KIDS SHOULD KNOW

"Python for Kids: A Fun and Easy Introduction to Programming"

Copyright © 2022 by Alvin. A Hiers

All rights reserved.

No portion of this book may be reproduced in any form without written permission from the publisher or author, except as permitted by U.S. copyright law.

TABLE OF CONTENT

I. Introduction to progam and programming language_____4

II. Introduction to Python and setting up a development environment_____6

III. Basic programming concepts such as variables, data types, and control structures_____41

IV. Working with strings and lists_____43

V. Defining and calling functions_____51

VI. Using modules and libraries_____53

VII. Handling errors and exceptions_____55

VIII. Rules in python programming_____59

INTRODUCTION

Welcome to the wonderful world of Python programming! This book is designed for kids who are interested in learning how to code. Python is a powerful, yet easy-to-learn programming language that is widely used in the industry. It is a great choice for beginners because it has a simple and straightforward syntax, which makes it easy to understand and write code. With this book, you will learn the basics of Python programming and gain the skills to create your own programs. You will be amazed at what you can do with just a few lines of code. So grab your computer, and let's get started on an exciting journey of discovery and creativity!

This book is designed to make learning to code fun and interactive. The concepts and examples covered in this book will help you understand the basic building blocks of programming and how they work together to create a complete program. You will be introduced to key Python features and concepts, including data types, control structures, functions, and modules. Along the way, you will also learn how to debug and test your code, making sure it runs correctly. With each chapter, you will build on your knowledge and skills, and by the end of the book, you will be ready to create your own Python programs.

CHAPTER ONE

What is a program ?

A program is a set of instructions that a computer can execute in order to perform a specific task or set of tasks. Programs are typically written in a programming language, which is then translated into machine code that the computer can understand and execute.

There are many different types of programs, each designed for a specific purpose. For example, there are operating systems like Windows and macOS, which provide the basic infrastructure for running other programs on a computer. There are also application programs, such as word processors and games, which are designed to perform specific tasks for users.

A program can be as simple as a single line of code, or as complex as a large suite of software with millions of lines of code.

In general, a program is a logical sequence of instructions that enable a computer to perform specific task.

What is programming language ?

A programming language is a set of instructions and rules that are used to create a software program. It is a way for humans to communicate with computers and to tell them what to do. There are many different programming languages, each with their own set of commands and syntax, and each is suited for different types of tasks. Some examples of popular programming languages include C, C++, Java, Python, JavaScript, and C#. Each language has its own strengths and weaknesses and is used in different types of applications, such as web development, mobile app development, desktop software, and machine learning.

A programmer writes code in a programming language, and then a compiler or interpreter translates that code into machine code, which is the language that a computer can understand and execute.

Programming languages also vary in their level of abstraction from the computer architecture, with some being high-level languages, which are easier for humans to read and write, and others being low-level languages, which are closer to the machine summary,

Programming Language is a medium of instruction for computers to execute a set of instructions, its like natural languages like English, French etc but designed to give instructions to computers.

Advantages of python programming languages

There are many advantages of using the Python programming language, including:

- **Easy to read and understand:** Python code is easy to read and understand, making it a great language for beginners. The language uses a simple syntax and has a relatively small set of keywords, making it easy to learn.

- **Highly versatile:** Python is a versatile language that can be used for a wide range of tasks, including web development, scientific computing, data analysis, artificial intelligence, and more.

- **Large and active community:** Python has a large and active community, which means that there is a wealth of resources available to help you learn the language and find solutions to problems.

- **Many libraries and frameworks:** Python has a large number of libraries and frameworks available, which makes it easy to perform complex tasks without having to write a lot of code from scratch.

- **Good for rapid development:** Python's interpreted nature, dynamically-typed and easy-to-learn syntax makes it a good choice for rapid development, as it allows for quick iteration and experimentation.

- **Platform independent:** Python can run on a wide range of platforms, including Windows, macOS, and Linux, as well as on devices such as Raspberry Pi and IoT devices, this makes it a good choice for writing cross-platform code.

- **High-level language:** Python is a high-level programming language, which means that it abstracts away many of the complex details of the computer and provides a simpler interface to the programmer.

- **Popular and in demand:** Python is one of the most popular and in-demand programming languages in the world. It is used in a wide range of industries, including finance, healthcare, technology, and more.These are some of the advantages of using the Python programming language. However, as with any programming language, it may not be the best fit for every situation and project.

Exercise 1

1. What is a program ?
2. What is programming language ?
3. List 5 advantages of python programming

CHAPTER TWO

Introduction to Python and setting up a development environment

What is python ?

Python is a high-level, interpreted programming language. It was created by Guido van Rossum in 1991 and is often used for web development, scientific computing, data analysis, artificial intelligence, and other advanced applications.

One of the key features of Python is its readability. Python code is designed to be easy to read and write, with a clear and consistent syntax that is easy to learn. This makes it an ideal language for beginners and experts alike.

Another feature that makes Python popular is its vast ecosystem of libraries and frameworks. These tools make it easy to perform many common programming tasks without having to write a lot of code from scratch. This saves developers time and makes their work more efficient.

Python is a general-purpose language, it means that it can be used for various types of applications such as web development, desktop applications, scientific computing, and artificial intelligence. Python is an interpreted language, which means that you don't need to manually compile your code before running it. This allows for quick and easy prototyping.

Overall, Python is a popular and versatile programming language that is widely used in industry and academia for its readability, ease of use, and powerful libraries and frameworks.

Setting up our python

programming environment

Python is a powerful programming language that is easy to learn and use. It is a great language for beginners, and it can be used for a wide variety of tasks, from simple scripts to complex programs. In this guide, we'll learn how to set up a development environment for Python and start writing our first Python programs.

First, let's talk about what a development environment is. A development environment is a place where you can write, test, and debug your code. It typically includes a text editor, which is where you'll write your code, and a way to run your code, such as a command line interface or an integrated development environment (IDE).

To start writing Python code, you'll need to have Python installed on your computer. You can download the latest version of Python from the official Python website, https://www.python.org/downloads/. Make sure to download the version that is appropriate for your computer's operating system. Once you have Python installed, you can start writing and running Python programs.

Now, let's set up a development environment. One popular development environment for Python is IDLE.

IDLE comes pre-installed with Python, so you don't have to download anything extra. To start IDLE, you can simply search for "IDLE" in your computer's start menu or launch it from the command prompt (in windows: press Win + R and type 'idle' and press Enter)

When IDLE launches, you'll see a new window with the Python Shell. This is where you can enter Python commands and see the results immediately. You can use this shell to test out small pieces of code and learn how Python works. To write a more complex program, you can click on "File" and then "New File" to create a new file where you can write your code.

Python uses indentation (whitespaces at the beginning of line) to indicate the structure of a program. So make sure that you maintain correct indentation.

You can also run your python programs through command prompt (Windows: Press Win + R and type 'cmd' and press Enter) and navigate to the directory where your python file is located and run your program by typing 'python file_name.py'

Congratulations! You now have a working Python development environment and you're ready to start writing your first Python program. A good way to start learning Python is by doing some interactive tutorials. These will help you learn the basics of the language and get you comfortable with the development environment.

Let's start with a simple program:

Print ("Hello, World!")

Figure 1.0

Figure 1.0 shows python environment with the command statement : print("Hello World")

This program uses the print function to output the string "Hello, World!" to the screen. You can run this program by saving it in a file with the ".py" file extension, and then running it using python or IDLE

Hope you have fun exploring Python and all the things you can create with it!

In Python, as in most programming languages, variables are used to store data. A variable is simply a name that refers to a value stored in the computer's memory. In Python, you can create a variable by giving it a name and assigning a value to it using the assignment operator (=). For example:

Copy code

x = 5

y = "Hello, world!"

In this example, x is a variable that holds the value 5, and y is a variable that holds the string

"Hello, world!".

Variables and data type in python programming language

There are several data types in Python that can be stored in variables. Some of the most commonly used data types are:

Integers: whole numbers, such as 1, 2, and 3.

Floating-point numbers: numbers with a decimal point, such as 3.14.

Strings: a sequence of characters, such as "hello" or "goodbye". Strings can be enclosed in either single or double quotes.

Booleans: represent true/false values, such as True or False

Lists: ordered collections of items, such as [1, , 3]

Dictionaries: collections of key-value pairs, such as {"a": 1, "b": 2}

Python also has several control structures that allow you to control the flow of a program. These include:

if-else statements: used to execute a block of code if a certain condition is true, and another block of code if the condition is false. For example:

x = 5

if x > 0:

   print("x is positive")

else:

   print("x is not positive")

for loops: used to iterate over a sequence of items, such as a list or a string. For example:

Copy code

for i in range(5):   print(i)

while loops: used to repeatedly execute a block of code as long as a certain condition is true. For example:

x = 5

while x > 0:

  print(x)

  x -= 1

It is also important to note that indentation is used to indicate which statements are inside a block of code in python. So in above example, the print statements are inside the if and else block as they are indented under them.

These are just a few of the basic concepts that are used in programming with Python. With these building blocks, you can start writing simple programs and gradually build up to more complex applications.

Integers

In Python, an integer (also called "int") is a whole number (positive, negative, or zero) that can be represented without a fractional component. For example, the numbers -1, 0, and 42 are all integers, while the numbers -1.5 and 3.14 are not.

In Python, integers are represented using the built-in "int" type. You can create an integer by assigning a value to a variable, or by using the int() function to convert a string or a floating-point number to an integer. For example:

x = 42

y = int("123")

z = int(4.6)

print(x, y, z) # prints "42 123 4"

The last example will truncate the decimal part of 4.6, while the middle example will convert the string "123" to an integer.

Integers have a range of values they can take up, which is platform dependent, Generally they are 32 bit or 64 bit, This means that on a machine with 32-bit integers, the largest representable integer is $(2^{31})-1$ and the smallest representable integer is $-(2^{31})$.

You can perform various arithmetic operations on integers such as addition, subtraction, multiplication, division, modulus and many more.

Figure 2.0

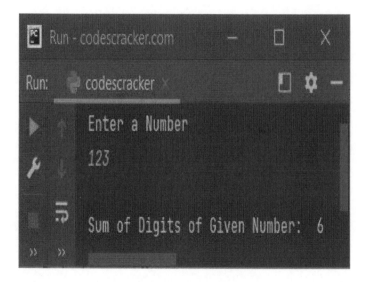

Figure 2.0 shows command on integers.

Strings

In Python, a string is a sequence of characters. It can be defined using single quotes ('...') or double quotes ("..."). For example:

string1 = 'Hello, world!'

```
string1 = 'Hello,
world!'
string2 = "This is a
string."
```

String2 = "This is a string."

You can also use the triple quotes ('''...''' or """...""") to create a multi-line string. For example:

String3 = '''This is a multi-line string."

```
string3 = '''This is
a multi-line
string.'''

string4 = """This is
also
a multi-line
string."""
```

String4 = """This is also

a multi-line

string."""

You can access individual characters in a string using indexing. The indexing starts from 0, so the first character in the string has index 0, the second character has index 1, and so on. For example:

(string1[0])   # prints 'H'

print(string1[7])   # prints 'w'

```
print(string1[0])   # prints 'H'
print(string1[7])   # prints 'w'
```

You can also use negative indexing to access characters from the end of the string. For example:

```
print(string1[-1])  # prints '!'

print(string1[-5])  # prints 'w'
```

You can use slicing to extract a portion of a string. For example, the following code extracts the substring "world" from the string "Hello, world!":

```
print(string1[7:12])   # prints 'world'
```

Python also provide several built-in method for string manipulation, Some of them like:

.upper()

.lower()

.replace()

.strip()

.split()

and many more you can check them by calling help('str') in your python console

And also, you can use the + operator to concatenate strings, and the * operator to repeat a string a certain number of times. For example:

string5 = string1 + ', how are you?'

print(string5) # prints "Hello, world!, how are you?"

string6 = string1 * 3

print(string6) # prints "Hello, world!Hello, world!Hello,world!"

```
string5 = string1 + ',
how are you?'
print(string5)   #
prints "Hello, world!,
how are you?"

string6 = string1 * 3
print(string6)   #
prints "Hello,
world!Hello,
world!Hello, world!"
```

Boolean statement

In Python, a Boolean statement is a statement that is either true or false. Boolean values in Python are represented by the keywords True and False. Boolean expressions, which are expressions that evaluate to a Boolean value, can be used to control the flow of a program. For example, an if statement is a common control flow construct that uses a Boolean expression to determine whether a certain block of code should be executed.

You can also use comparison operator(like ==, > , <, !=, >=, <=) to get Boolean value as comparison return Boolean.

You can also use logical operator(like and, or, not) to combine multiple Boolean expressions and return a single Boolean value.

For example:

x = 5

y = 10

print(x == y) # False

print(x > y) # False

print(x < y) # True

```
x = 5
y = 10
print(x == y) # False
print(x > y) # False
print(x < y) # True
```

Lists

In Python, a list is a collection of items that are ordered and changeable. Lists are written with square brackets and the items are separated by commas. For example:

my_list = [1, 2, 3, 4, 5]

This creates a list called my_list containing the integers 1, 2, 3, 4, and 5. Lists can contain any type of data, including other lists, and can be modified by adding, removing, or changing items.

```
my_list = [1, 2, 3, 4, 5]
```

my_list.append(6)   # this adds 6 to the end of the list

my_list.remove(4)   # this removes the 4 from the list

my_list[2] = 9   # this changes the 3rd item in the list to 9

```python
my_list.append(6)    #
this adds 6 to the
end of the list
my_list.remove(4)    #
this removes the 4
from the list
my_list[2] = 9       #
this changes the 3rd
item in the list to
9
```

Lists are one of the most commonly used data types in Python, and are widely used in many types of programming, including web development, data analysis, and scientific computing.

Dictionaries

In Python, a dictionary is a data structure that stores items as key-value pairs. The keys are used to access the associated values, and must be unique within the dictionary. The values can be of any data type and can be duplicated. Dictionaries are also often called associative arrays, maps, or hash maps in other programming languages. Dictionaries are defined using curly braces {} and colons :

Example:

```
my_dict = {'key1': 'value1', 'key2': 'value2', 'key3': 'value3'}
```

my_dict = {'key1': 'value1', 'key2': 'value2', 'key3': 'value3'}

You can also initialize an empty dictionary using empty_dict = {}

You can access the elements of a dictionary by referencing its key:

```
>>> my_dict['key4'] = 'value4'
>>> my_dict
{'key1': 'value1',
 'key2': 'value2',
 'key3': 'value3',
 'key4': 'value4'}
>>> del my_dict['key1']
>>> my_dict
{'key2': 'value2',
 'key3': 'value3',
 'key4': 'value4'}
>>> my_dict['key2']
```

```
>>> del my_dict['key1']
>>> my_dict
{'key2': 'value2',
 'key3': 'value3',
 'key4': 'value4'}
>>> my_dict['key2'] = 'new_value'
>>> my_dict
{'key2': 'new_value', 'key3': 'value3', 'key4': 'value4'}
```

>>> my_dict = {'key1': 'value1', 'key2': 'value2', 'key3': 'value3'}

>>> my_dict['key1']

'value1'

You can add, remove or update the elements of

dictionary by assignment

>>> my_dict['key4'] = 'value4'

>>> my_dict

{'key1': 'value1', 'key2': 'value2', 'key3': 'value3', 'key4': 'value4'}

>>> del my_dict['key1']

>>> my_dict

{'key2': 'value2', 'key3': 'value3', 'key4': 'value4'}

>>> my_dict['key2'] = 'new_value'

>>> my_dict

{'key2': 'new_value', 'key3': 'value3', 'key4': 'value4'}

Dictionary keys must be immutable. Meaning you can use strings, numbers, or tuples as keys but lists, for example, are not immutable and cannot be used as keys.

If-else statement

In Python, an "if-else" statement is a control flow statement that allows the programmer to specify a block of code to be executed if a certain condition is true, and a different block of code to be executed if the condition is false. The basic syntax of an if-else statement is as follows:

```
if condition:
    # code to be executed if condition is true
else:
    # code to be executed if condition is false
```

if condition:

   # code to be executed if condition is true

else:

   # code to be executed if condition is false

The condition is an expression that evaluates to either True or False. If the condition is true, the code in the if block is executed; otherwise, the code in the else block is executed.

For example:

Copy code

x = 5 ,if x > 0:

```
x = 5
if x > 0:
    print("x is positive")
else:
    print("x is not positive")
```

print("x is positive")

else:

print("x is not positive")

the output will be "x is positive"

You can chain multiple if-else statements as well called if-elif-else.

Copy code

```
if condition1:
    # code to be executed if condition1 is true
elif condition2:
    # code to be executed if condition1 is false and condition2 is true
else:
    # code to be executed if both condition1 and condition2 are false
```

```python
if condition1:
    # code to be executed if condition1 is true
elif condition2:
    # code to be executed if condition1 is false and condition2 is true
else:
    # code to be executed if both
```

Excerise 2

1. What is python programming language ?
2. List two steps in setting up python programming language environment
3. List 5 data types in python programming
4. What is if-else statement ?
5. How can strings be used in python
6. List 3 Examples of integers

CHAPTER THREE

Basic programming concepts such as variables, data types, and control structures

In Python, some basic programming concepts include:

Variables: a container that stores a value, which can be a number, a string, or other types of data. Variables are assigned a value using the assignment operator (=).

For example:

x = 5

name = "John"

Data types
: the kind of value a variable holds. Python has several built-in data types including numbers (int, float), strings, lists, and dictionaries.

For example:

x = 5 (x is integer)

name = "John" (name is string)

Control structures:
are used to control the flow of execution of a program. Python has several control structures including:

if-else: used for conditional execution of code

for/while: used for looping over a block of code

try-except: used for error handling

Functions : They are a way to organize code, it helps with reusability, readability and grouping related code

Classes: They are a blueprint of objects and encapsulate data and functions together.

Working with strings and lists

In Python, strings are sequences of characters and are used to represent text. They are enclosed in either single quotes (') or double quotes ("), and can be manipulated using various built-in methods and operators. For example, you can use the + operator to concatenate two strings, or the len() function to get the length of a string.

Lists are also a built-in data structure in Python. They are used to store an ordered collection of items, which can be of any type. Lists are enclosed in square brackets ([]), and items in a list are separated by commas. For example, a list of integers could be written as [1, 2, 3], and a list of strings could be written as ["a", "b", "c"]. You can access individual items in a list by their index, which starts at 0. you can use list methods like append() ,extend() and pop() to add and remove elements. list comprehension can also be used with list.

Both strings and lists are iterable in python, which means you can use them in loops and other operations that can be applied to iterable objects.

Here are some examples of working with strings and lists in Python:

Strings:

Concatenating strings

name = "John"

age = 25

print("My name is " + name + " and I am " + str(age) + "

years old.")

String formatting

print("My name is {} and I am {} years old.".format(name, age))

String interpolation (Python 3.6+)

print(f"My name is {name} and I am {age} years old.")

String methods

s = "Hello, World!"

print(s.upper())   # "HELLO, WORLD!"

print(s.lower())   # "hello, world!"

print(s.strip())   # "Hello, World!"

print(s.replace("H", "J"))   # "Jello, World!"

```python
# Concatenating strings
name = "John"
age = 25
print("My name is " + name + " and I am " + str(age) + " years old.")

# String formatting
print("My name is {} and I am {} years old.".format(name,
```

```python
# String formatting
print("My name is {} and I am {} years old.".format(name, age))

# String interpolation (Python 3.6+)
print(f"My name is {name} and I am {age} years old.")

# String methods
```

```python
# String methods
s = "Hello, World!"
print(s.upper())      # "HELLO, WORLD!"
print(s.lower())      # "hello, world!"
print(s.strip())      # "Hello, World!"
print(s.replace("H", "J"))   # "Jello, World!"
```

Lists:

Creating a list

fruits = ["apple", "banana", "cherry"]

Accessing elements in a list

print(fruits[0])   # "apple"

print(fruits[-1])   # "cherry"

```python
# Modifying elements in a list
fruits[1] = "mango"


# Iterating over a list
for fruit in fruits:
    print(fruit)


# List slicing
fruits = ["apple", "banana", "cherry", "date","elder","fig"]
print(fruits[1:3])    # ["banana", "cherry"]
print(fruits[:3])     # ["apple", "banana", "cherry"]
print(fruits[3:])     # ["date","elder","fig"]
```

```python
# Creating a list
fruits = ["apple", "banana", "cherry"]

# Accessing elements in a list
print(fruits[0])    # "apple"
print(fruits[-1])   # "cherry"

# Modifying elements in a list
fruits[1] = "mango"

# Iterating over a list
for fruit in fruits:
    print(fruit)
```

```python
        print(fruit)

# List slicing
fruits = ["apple", "banana", "cherry", "date","elder","fig"]
print(fruits[1:3])
# ["banana", "cherry"]
print(fruits[:3])    # ["apple", "banana", "cherry"]
print(fruits[3:])    # ["date","elder","fig"]
```

Defining and calling functions

In Python, a function is a block of code that can be reused multiple times in a program. A function is defined using the def keyword, followed by the name of the function, a set of parentheses, and a colon. The code block within the function is indented underneath.

For example, here is a simple function named greet that takes in a single argument, a name, and prints out a greeting:

def greet(name):

  print("Hello, " + name + "!")

A function can be called by using its name followed by a set of parentheses and any arguments that the function takes in. For example, the greet function could be called as follows:

greet("John")

Output: Hello, John!

Functions can also return a value using the return keyword, like this :

```
def add(a, b):
    return a + b


result = add(1, 2)
print(result)
# Output: 3
```

It is defining the function called add which takes two argument a,b and return the sum of a and b, this can be stored in any variable to use it again.

Modules in python programming

In Python, modules are files containing definitions and statements. A module can define functions, classes, and variables, and can also include runnable code. By using the import statement, you can use the definitions and statements from a module in your program.

For example, you can use the built-in math module in your program by importing it using the following statement:

import math

After importing the module, you can use its functions and variables by referencing them with the module name, separated by a dot. For example, you can use the math.sqrt() function to find the square root of a number:

x = math.sqrt(16)

print(x)

output

4.0

A library is a collection of modules that you can use to perform a variety of tasks. The Python Standard Library is a collection of modules that are included with Python, and provide a wide range of functionality, from working with data, to interacting with the operating system, to working with network sockets, to manipulating text.

There are many third-party libraries available for use in Python, which you can install and import into your programs. You can install these libraries with package managers like pip, conda.

For example, if you want to use the popular pandas library for working with data in your program, you can install it using pip and then import it:

!pip install pandas

import pandas as pd

Once you have installed the library and imported it into your program, you can use its functions and classes in your code.

Handling errors and exceptions in python programming

In Python, errors and exceptions are handled using try-except blocks. The try block contains the code that might raise an exception, and the except block contains the code that will be executed in case an exception is raised. If an exception is raised in the try block and not caught by any except block, the program will terminate.

For example:

try:

  # some code here

  x = 1/0

except ZeroDivisionError:

  print("division by zero")

Here, the try block contains the statement x = 1/0,

which raises a ZeroDivisionError exception. The except block catches this exception and prints a message.

You can also use the finally block, it will run the code regardless whether exception is thrown or not after try and except block.

try:

   # some code here

   x = 1/0

except ZeroDivisionError:

   print("division by zero")

finally:

   print("this will run always")

You can also handle multiple exception at once by

try:

   # some code here

   x = 1/0

```
except (ZeroDivisionError, TypeError, ValueError):
    print("exception occured")
```

You also have else block which will run when no exception occurs in try block

```
try:
    # some code here
    x = 1/0
except ZeroDivisionError:
    print("division by zero")
else:
    print("no exception occured")
```

You can also raise an exception in case of specific conditions, by using raise keyword.

```
if x < 0:
    raise ValueError("x should be positive")
```

It is also possible to define custom exception classes by subclassing the Exception class, and then raise instances of the custom exception class.

It's always good practice to handle errors and exceptions whenever there's a possibility of an error, to ensure your program does not terminate unexpectedly, and can handle errors in a meaningful way.

Rules in python programming

Here are some basic rules for writing valid Python code:

1. Python is case-sensitive, so make sure to use the correct case for variable, function, and class names.

2. Python uses indentation to indicate code blocks, so make sure to indent your code correctly.

3. Python uses colons (:) to indicate the start of a code block, and the end of a code block is indicated by the lack of indentation.

4. Python uses the standard mathematical operators (+, -, *, /, %) for addition, subtraction, multiplication, division, and modulus.

5. Python uses parentheses to group expressions and control the order of operations.

6. Python uses the double equal sign (==) to test for equality, and the single equal sign (=) to assign a value to a variable.

7. Python uses the keywords 'and', 'or' and 'not' for logical operations.

8. Python uses the keywords 'if', 'elif' and 'else' for conditional statements.

9. Python uses the keywords 'for' and 'while' for loops.

10. Comments in python are written with a pound sign (#)

These are some of the basic rules that you should keep in mind when writing Python code. Remember that practice is the key to becoming a proficient Python programmer.

Exercise 3

1. What is a variable
2. What are data types
3. List 3 examples of modules
4. List 6 rules in python programming

Conclusion

"The Python Programming your kids should know "is an excellent resource for young learners to begin their journey into the world of coding. Through interactive examples and easy-to-understand explanations, this book provides a solid foundation for kids to build their programming skills. As they work through the exercises and projects, they will gain confidence in their ability to create and customize their own programs. I highly recommend this book to any parent or educator looking to introduce their children to the exciting field of computer programming."

Printed in France by Amazon
Brétigny-sur-Orge, FR